ALEKSANDR ORLOV

PRESENTS

YAKOV

Saves Christmas

**MEERKAT CLASSICS**

RUSSIA 2012

Yakov Saves Christmas
**ALEKSANDR ORLOV**

1 3 5 7 9 10 8 6 4 2

First published in 2012 by Ebury Press, an imprint of Ebury Publishing

A Random House Group company

This is an advertisement feature on behalf of comparethemarket.com

comparethemeerkat.com and comparethemarket.com
are trading names of BISL Limited

The Random House Group Limited Reg. No. 954009

Addresses for companies within the Random House Group can be found at www.randomhouse.co.uk

A CIP catalogue record for this book is available from the British Library

The Random House Group Limited supports The Forest Stewardship Council (FSC®), the leading international forest certification organisation. Our books carrying the FSC label are printed on FSC® certified paper. FSC is the only forest certification scheme endorsed by the leading environmental organisations, including Greenpeace. Our paper procurement policy can be found at www.randomhouse.co.uk/environment

MIX
Paper from
responsible sources
FSC® C013123

Printed and bound in Italy by Graphicom SRL

ISBN 9780091950019

To buy books by your favourite authors and register for offers visit
www.randomhouse.co.uk

This is a work of fiction. Names and characters are the product of the author's imagination and any resemblance to actual persons, living or dead, is entirely coincindental

# A MESSAGE FROM THE AUTHOR

Welcome to this special festive bookamabob from the world of Meerkovo!

This story is all about Yakov, our beloved Meerkat Elder. He is also favourite of meerpups because he is full of wisdom and kindness and, most important, makes beautiful toys in his beautiful toyshop.

He is very much admired, even though he is not in the first flushings of his youth (like another elderly Meerkovian we could mention. But let's not talk about Sergei, or his head will get all big and he will not have time to mend my computermabob).

Here is Yakov's thrillsy story. It is very Christmassy and perfect for read by fire after festive meal of roast scarab beetle.

Please be enjoyings.

Yours,

ALEKSANDR ORLOV

Somewhere near the North Pole*, where it is very freezey and full of snowings and iciness, there is an **enormous workshop.**

Hidden by high mountains, it cover huge area and is made of brightly painted wood. This make it very cheerful, plus little wood mites provide extra source of nourishment.
It is very secret workshop, but we are going to look inside.

NORTH POLE

*This is the one at the top if you are looking at the world from the bottom.

When we open the door we see many, many muskrat elves. They are small and elf-like and they are scurry about very quickly on their tiny paws. Some are putting cuddly toys in boxes. Some are wrapping up sugar-coated grubs in brightly coloured paper. And some are tying up brown paper parcels with string.

In the middle of them all is piles and piles of letters to Santa Claws from meerpups all over the world. One is pile for good pups (this is biggest pile), another for quite good pups, and then there is small one for naughty pups*. It is very difficult sorting job, but the elves are **very clever at it** and don't make mistakes.

Dear Santa Claws
I would like
a bright red
racing car like
this one →
from
Bogdan

It may be his best handwriting, but I think little Bogdan is push his luck here!

*I'm sure you are not naughty pup, but if you were you would still get present from Santa. Just not a very big one.

Everywhere there is scurry, for Christmas is only hours away and the world's meerkats and meerpups will need their presents.

In among them all, there is Santa Claws. He is **very big and red and looking full of sweatiness.**\*

Next to him is Chief Toy-Maker Yakov. He is very calm and is making sure all the toys are perfect and everything run smooth.

Santa's favourite reindeer clock show how fast time is ticking down to Christmas.

\*This can be sign of ill health. Sergei was full of sweatiness not long ago and the next thing we knew he was hospital!

Suddenly there is huge **bang**. Everyone look round at place where Santa Claws was stand. He has passed out because of all the sweatiness and fallen over! He is lying on floor with his tummy pointing upwards. It is big tummy (perhaps because of all those cricket cookies he eats when he makes deliveries), and when he come to, he is full of queasiness and cannot get up.

# All the little elves start to panic.

The air is full of chatter and alarm.

But Chief Toy-Maker Yakov climbs on top of a box of Knightkat magazines and asks for calm. "Please," he says. "Be calm. We must finish our work, the meerpups of the world depend on us."

He is a meerkat of few words but quiet authority, and soon the chattering is quieten.

They all make Santa Claws comfortables on the floor, but now there is **terrible emergencies** because who will do the toy delivering?

There is only one who can save the day. All the little elves look hopefully at him...

*I think Santa will be better with all this comforting. (Pack include his special Stomach-Settling Pills).*

Yakov, Chief Toy-Maker, drew himself up to his full height (which did not take long as Yakov not very tall) and with all his calmness he announce that he will undertake to do all the toy delivery.

So then the elves are back packing sacks. They sing their famous Sack-Packing Song as they go.

## "Hi diddley-doo, hi diddley-dee,

it's a sack-packer's life for me!" they yell merrily, rather out of tune.*

*It isn't actually a very famous song because they are secret elves. But they hope it will be famousness when they win big talent contest.

Yakov then wakes up Stanislovskivich*, the Chief Reindeer, who was having a nap because he knew he had a long night ahead of him. Yakov told him to get all the reindeers ready to pull the sleigh. **They were much later setting off than usual,** so they have to be quickness.

*Stanislovskivich's real name was Stan. But he lengthened himself when he was made Chief Reindeer.

The elves lined up to wish Yakov luck.
# "Good luck," they cried.

Then they were off. Yakov, dressed in Santa Claws's
spare red suit (it was a bit big for him but he was glad of
extra bulky because it was cold), held tight to the reindeer
reins as the sleigh went up, up, up and away in the sky.

Santa's suit is built for freeziness.
Even his designer underwear
is double thermalled!

# "First stop Africa!" shouted Yakov above the noise
of sleigh turbulence.

They swooped down and with incredible swiftness visited
burrow after burrow in all the deserts, delivering presents as they
went. Sometimes they had a hasty cricket cookie, sometimes a cup
of beetle juice, but mostly they were rushing.

# "Asia next!" cried Yakov to his trusty reindeer team.
Asia was very busy, with lots and lots of homes and many meerpups.
They were running out of time, so they didn't stop for cookies.

Santa's route change every year according to wind.
I think this Christmas was extra windy!

# "And now for the rest of the world,"

said Yakov, by now a little exhaustipated. Off they flew. Stan was strong and brave, and so were his friends, which was lucky because there were many countries in the rest of the world. This time they stopped for an occasional American Aphid Cookie and a Fried French Frog-leg. It was hungry work, all this delivering, but they couldn't stop for long.

French frog-legs are absolute deliciousness – sometimes I even give box to Sergei if he has work extra hard.

Finally, it was time for the last country, Russia. By now, everyone was very tiredness, so Yakov stood on the sleigh seat and gave a little speech to encourage – "Once more unto the sky, dear friends, once more"* he said.

Off they went, strengthened by Yakov's words and cups of warm mouse milk. Then just as **Christmas Eve was turn into Christmas Day** they finish delivering everyone's presents and get home to the North Pole. Thank goodness, they all thought (they were too tired to speak).

---

*Yakov is rather scholarly and full of oratory. If you are swotkat, you will recognise where this quote come from.

Yakov was falling asleep at the reins. He rubbed his eyes because he knew you shouldn't sleep at the reins – and listened to the jingly bells on his sleigh. Jingle, jingle, they went, and then boom and clang. What was this? They weren't sleigh bells at all, they were church bells –

# it was **Christmas Morning!**

This is Meerkovo church bell. It is called Big Ant after my Papa Anton.

Yakov opened his eyes and found himself in his toy shop, lying underneath his carved wooden Christmas tree. He felt so sleepy. Perhaps he had been dreaming. But as he looked at his tree, he saw a large sparkly parcel. It had a little note attached. It said: "Happy Christmas. And thank you. Santa Claws".

# Aleksandr's Life Lesson

When all around is panic, you can do most good if you keep your head on.

# Now read my other greatest tales

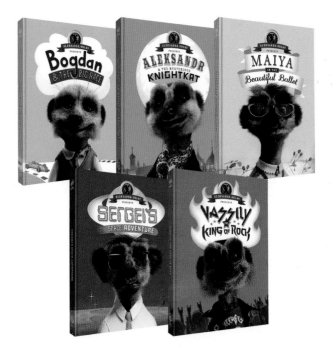

## Available from all good bookshops

Also available to download as an ebookamabob
or audiomajig as read by the author – me!

For more information visit www.comparethemeerkat.com